# HTML For Beginners

Joseph Jossy

# DEDICATION

This book is dedicated to everybody that wants to learn HTML

# CONTENTS

# What is HTML

HTML stands for Hypertext markup language. HTML is a markup language for building webpages.
HTML is made up of 2 main sections.

- The Head Section.
The Body Section.

# HTML Editor

There are so many HTML editors like Atom, Notepad++, Sublime text, and many more but I will advise you to use Visual Studio Code (VS code). VS code is one of the best code editors, it has a lovely beginner-friendly interface.

The Head Section: This is the section that contains all the metadata and information about the webpage. The head section is the first element on an HTML document. To install VS code, visit https://code.visualstudio.com and install it on your computer. It is available for Windows, Mac, and Linux operating systems. Once you install VS code, the next thing is to install some extensions inside your VS code, Click on the extension bar and search for those 2 extensions...

- **Prettier**: used for code formatting

- **Live Server**: used to launch a development local Server with

a live reload feature for static
& dynamic pages

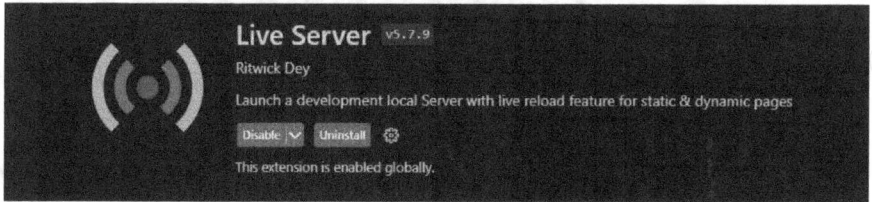

Once you install those 2
extensions, you are ready to
create your first HTML document.

# Creating An HTML Document

There are so many ways to create an HTML document but I will be teaching you how to make it inside your VS code. First, you need to create a folder in your computer where your files will be saved, then Open the folder in your VS code, Click on New file, and write the name of your file, the file extension must be .html, For example, I can name my file **Index.html** and press the **ENTER** key and my HTML file will be created.

# HTML Tags

HTML tags are those keywords that tell the browser how to format and display the content. HTML tags are categorized into two

- Paired tags
- Unpaired tags

**Paired tags** are tags with both opening and closing. A paired tag can have a child tag, plain text, or attitude. For example, <p>, <h1>, <div>.

**Unpaired tags** are tags with only an opening, they don't require a closing tag. For example <img>, <input>, <br>.

# List of Paired tags

Below is the list of some commonly used paired tags in HTML.

- \<html>: The \<html> element is the first tag in an HTML document after the DOCTYPE, it is the root element and it defines the whole HTML document.

- <head>: The head tag contains all the metadata and information about the webpage. This is also where you import external files like CSS and JavaScript
- <body>: The body contains all the contents in an HTML document, It Contains tags that are been displayed on the browser. There can only be one <body> tag.
- <h1>: The <h1> element is used to define the most important heading. The heading tags go from <h1> to <h6>. The <h6> is used to define the list of important

headings. The <h1> displays bigger text more than the <h2> and the <h2> displays more than the <h3> and so on.

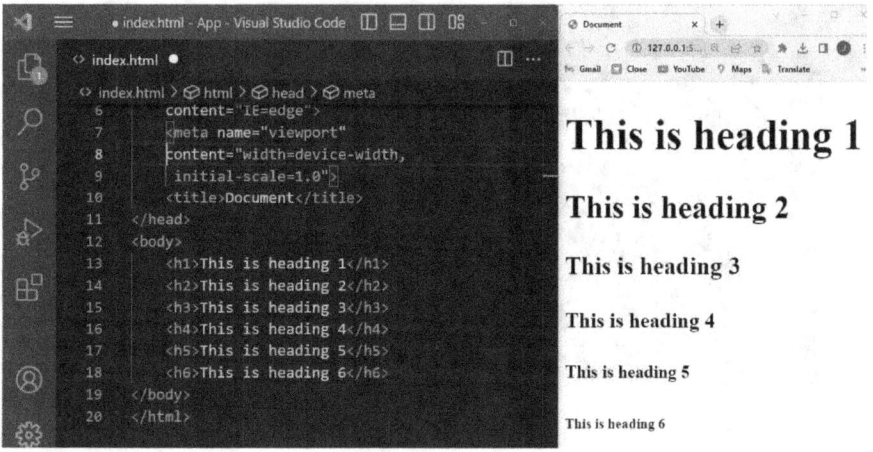

- <p>: The <p> tag represent a paragraph. Paragraph belongs to a class of elements called **Block-level elements.**
- <a>: used to link from one page to another.

- <div>: The <div> is used to make a division of content in HTML. The <div> tag is arguably the most used tag in HTML.

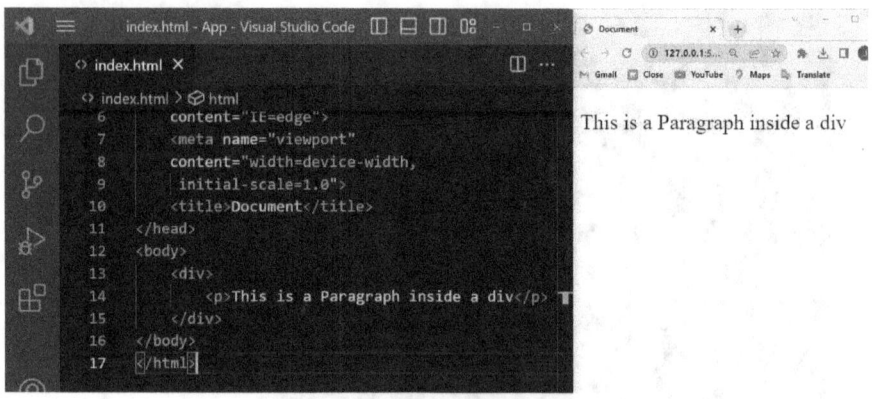

- <span>: The <Span> tag is similar to the <div>,It can be used as a container.
- <Section>: The <section> tag is used to create standalone sections within an HTML webpage.

- **<b>**: used to make text bold
- **<i>**: used to make the text italic
- **<u>**: used to underline a text

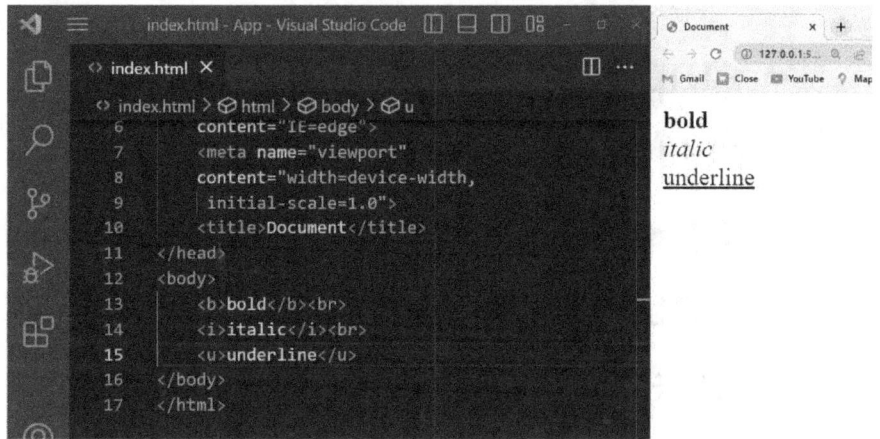

# List Of Unpaired Tags

Below is the list of unpaired tags in HTML…

- <input>: The <input> is an HTML tag that creates an input field where the user can input data, the <input> tag is mostly used within a <form> tag.
- <br>: The <br> tag is used to insert a line break in the text.
- <hr>: The <hr> tag defines a thematic break in an HTML document. It mostly displays a horizontal line in the web browser.

- <img>: The <Img> tag is used to insert an image in an HTML webpage. it takes in some attributes. Don't worry, we will learn about attributes in the next chapter.

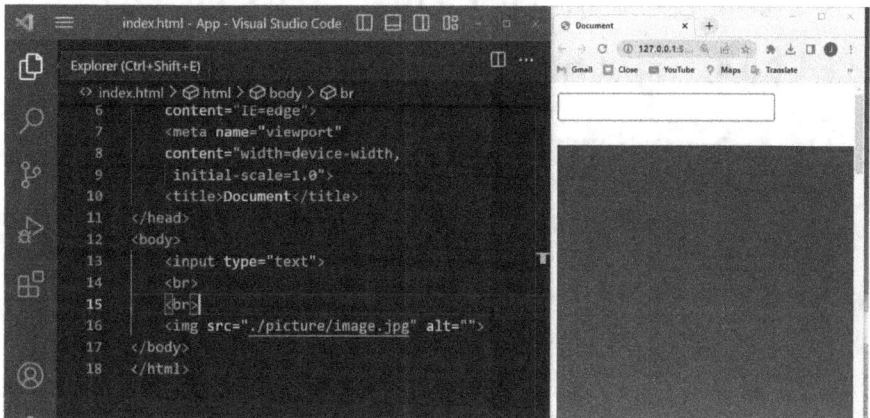

# Attributes In Html

HTML attributes are used inside an HTML tag to control the behavior of that element. It is used in the opening tag of an HTML element. Both paired and unpaired tags have there our attributes. some of the most used attributes in HTML are **"src"** which means **Source**, **"alt"**

which means **Alternative,** and **"href"** which means **Hyperlink Reference.**

# Comment In HTML

A comment tag is a tag used to insert a comment in HTML. A comment cannot be displayed in the web browser. The HTML comment tag is <!-- Your Comment --> . You can use the comment tag to remember where you stopped or used it to define the functionality of a section of code.

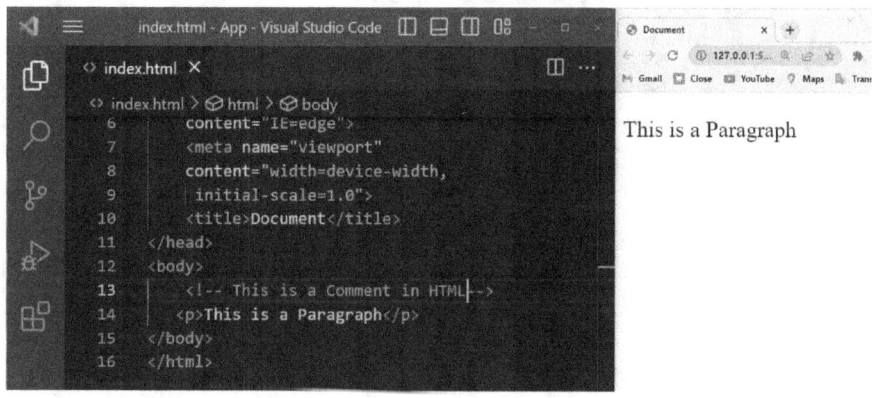

# Conclusion On HTML

HTML simply means Hypertext markup language, it defines the building structure of a webpage. Once you are done mastering HTML, the next step is to learn **CSS** which means **Cascading Style Sheets.** CSS is used for styling a webpage.

# ABOUT THE AUTHOR

My name is Joseph Jossy, I'm a front-end web developer, and I have 7 years of experience in front-end web development. I love Coding, Football, and writing books. I started my web development journey when I was 17 years old and I must say that I really enjoying the journey so far.